Prayers of An Angry Husband

Dedication: This book is written for every angry husband that didn't know how to pray whenever his wife got on his nerves, and for every husband who forgot to do his part and cover his wife in prayer. This book is also written to ensure that every husband, from this day forward, will know the proper way to pray for his wife even in the time she's annoying, moody, needy, loving, and even hurtful. This book is also dedicated to every woman who was not properly covered, may the man in your life cover you properly and consistently. The Scripture below gives direction for husbands to do all you can for your wife, so that your prayers will not be hindered.

1 Peter 3:7

7

Husbands, likewise, dwell with them with understanding, giving honor to the wife, as to the weaker vessel, and as being heirs together of the grace of life, that your prayers may not be hindered.

Prayer 1-

(What I prayed)- God, why is she getting on my nerves today? I don't feel like hearing her complain about the house not being clean. She has been home longer than I have and she had a long time to clean up. All I want is to chill right now and not be bothered.

(What I should've prayed)- God, I may be tired, but let me hear what my wife is saying to me. Let me be a help to her if there was too much burden on her today. Let me turn down my flesh and needs to cater to hers, you gave her to me as a helpmeet, and I am going to help. In Jesus name, Amen.

Devotional: Men, remember that your first responsibility is to love your wife as Christ loves the church and has done and will do anything for the church. That is how Christ has done for us; there are times when she needs you to do stuff, and as a loving husband, it is your duty to do for her anything she would need.

Prayer 2 – (What I prayed) God, is she really asking me why am I arguing with her? She isn't listening to anything that I am saying right now, and I don't even want to talk to her. I am getting sick and tired of her wanting to make all her points and don't want to hear anything I have to say.

(What I should've prayed)- GOD, let me take a minute so that I don't hurt my wife with harmful words. Let me take a second to listen to what she has to say as I pray that she takes a minute to hear me. Let me remember that she is my wife and I cannot raise my voice at her. GOD help us in our communication with each other and as the leader, let me know when to pause and direct us in a better direction. In Jesus name, Amen.

Devotional: Men, remember to use soft words when talking to your wife. Words have the power to kill and destroy, and although we may not get it right all the time because it is so easy to argue and yell back and forth, we have to remember that soft words go a long way. If you don't know how to use soft words when talking to your wife, then ask GOD to help you in that area. You can literally destroy your wife by your words and tone alone, and GOD expects to build our wives up not tear them down.

Prayer 3- (What I prayed) God, why does she think she can make decisions without consulting me? Here we have arrived, at another decision that affects our finances and our family and she wants me to be on board with this. Tired of making the same points about being a team when she was just trying to walk in her own way.

What I should've prayed)- God, as the leader of this home, let me hear clearly from you so that I know how to lead my wife. By my leading, make her understand the order of how you called the family structure. If I was out of your will, let us both walk in it so that we can get on the same team. Let me not be so quick to anger and try to understand her side of the story. In Jesus name, Amen.

Devotional: Men, GOD designed you to be head over the household and make household decisions. Once you make a decision outside the Will of GOD, or if you are not discerning the voice of GOD when He is giving your wife the Vision you

will miss out. It will be simply difficult for your wife to trust you in this area of leading the family and that will cause issues. Pray to GOD that He gives you the discernment necessary so that your wife never has to question those choices. Also, pray to know when GOD is giving your wife the Vision which is something He will do at times, and as the leader, you make that final decision, that is how you keep the peace in your home.

Prayer 4- (What I prayed) God, she is so damn hard headed and not listening to anything I am saying. We just left the doctor who told her to take it easy, and she is still trying to do too much. I have told her time and time again to just rest, take a break from her friends and social media, but she just won't listen. She keeps complaining about how tired she is but won't rest. Then, when I say something to her, she gets an attitude. I don't have time for this at all; I am doing my part.

(What I should've prayed)- God, speak to Your daughter so that she can rest. Let her trust me as her husband that You sent me here to help take care of her. You are the God who heals, so I pray that You heal my wife. As her husband, it hurts for me to see her like this, but I just need her to slow down. Her health means so much to me, and I wish to show her that taking a break is so essential for healing.

Devotional: Men, remember that one of your vows is in sickness and in health. If you have a wife that has any chronic disease or not feeling well, remember to stay in constant prayer for her, even if it's difficult at times. As a husband, you have to stay in constant prayer, and as stated before, any negative words or emotions can affect how your wife feels. There were times in my marriage alone where I dropped the ball in this area knowing that at times she may not have been feeling her best, it would have helped me more to stay in continual prayer instead of complaining about what she wasn't doing.

Prayer 5- (What I prayed) God, she said today that I bring out the rage in her. Well, doesn't she know that she brings out the rage in me? God, why can't You just show her what she is doing and how she is affecting me? God, why can't You fix her? Clearly, she needs to be fixed. I am doing everything on my end that I can do, she needs to fix her end.

(What I should've prayed) – God, what am I doing to bring out the rage in her? What am I doing as the husband and leader that makes her react like that? God, show us as a team what things we are doing to cause each other frustration? In the name of Jesus, I rebuke the enemy trying to attack our marriage. God, let our flesh die to You so that we can move out our way and You get the glory in our marriage.

Devotional: Men, I wonder how GOD feels at times when we make Him upset and bring out the anger in Him. I wonder how GOD feels when we go back and forth with Him on things we know better on. If negativity is the atmosphere in your home and you hear something like that, then you wonder what needs to be done in order to bring peace back into your home. You can allow peace to rain in your home, or you can allow destruction and confusion, and there were times when I didn't want to try and fix it the right way, just wanted to complain about how negative it was.

Prayer 6- (What I prayed) God, where is she when I need her? Why does she make me feel like I am alone in this marriage? When I voice to her the things that I think about, and she doesn't want to hear me. Doesn't she know that there are other women out there that will happily listen to my problems? What happened to her being my helpmeet? All I need for her to do is listen to what I am saying and how I feel.

(What I should've prayed) God, forgive me for being in my flesh and even thinking about another woman, that is the enemy, and I cannot break the

promise to You and please my flesh. God, help me show her why I need her there for me as my wife. I thank You for bringing her in my life, and I pray for us to get on the same page.

Devotional: Men, when you feel like you don't have a voice in your own home anymore, that's when you go to GOD to hear you. Never allow any outside influence or go complaining to other females. If it gets to the point where you feel like you have no one to talk to, it's ok to see a therapist. Couples Therapy is also an option as it relates to communication. GOD doesn't want you to feel that way in your own marriage, but there are options without involving anyone else, especially other women.

Prayer 7- (What I prayed) God, why did You give me this woman to marry? I know You said that he who finds a wife finds a good thing, but if this is marriage, I don't want it. I feel like she isn't even trying to get on the same page with me. Why am I wasting my time within this marriage?

(What I should've prayed) God, your word says he who finds a wife finds a good thing and gains favor from the lord. I rebuke myself for feeling this way. Remind me that she is my favor from You and I don't want to lose that favor from You. Show me how to speak her love language so that we can be on the same page. The enemy has tried to continually divide us in this manner and but God, I pray that You help us in this season.

Devotional: Men, as stated in the prayer, the bible tells us in Proverbs 18:22 that he who finds a wife finds a good thing and gains favor from the lord. GOD wants the best for your marriage, and even if it's not the person that He designed for you, because you made a vow to Him, you will gain favor. GOD gives us free will, and even if we believe it's the person He has for us, He expects us to hold our end of the bargain. So even when times get rough, and you just cannot stand your wife, do all you can to work it out with her and honor the vows you made to GOD. Just like Christ doesn't give up on the church (His bride) we can't give up so easy on ours.

Prayer 8- What I prayed) God, she really bumped her head if she thinks I am going to allow her to go out and not respond to me. How does she feel a married woman can just go out and come in just any time of the morning? She better respond to my text message, or when she comes in, I am going off.

(What I should've prayed) God, let my wife understand what I need as her husband. Let her realize that communication is a big part of marriage to me. I know she doesn't want to feel like I am "fathering her" but let her understand that I want to know she is always safe.

Devotional: Men, it is good to establish boundaries in your home and rules way before the marriage begins. I think a lot of times, we are so "in love" we do not set up necessary boundaries, and by the time we face an issue it is too late, and we begin to create a negative experience in our home. Find some time to sit down with your girlfriend/fiancé/spouse to talk about expectations on both ends as it relates to respectable times to come home. The women in your life have to understand that you aren't trying to give them a curfew, and you have to understand the women in your lives aren't trying to give you a curfew but coming in at a respectable time or having a thorough conversation about it will save you from a lot of unnecessary discord.

Prayer 9- (What I prayed) God, I am really going through a rough patch in my life, and I need her to be here for me. Why do I have to ask her to be here for me and for her undivided attention? She said I am too "needy at times" What in the hell is she talking about? This is exactly why I stopped coming to her with anything because when I do, I have to deal with this. I am tired God; I have nowhere to turn.

(What I should've prayed) GOD, I pray that she really takes the time to hear what I am saying.

Even if she is going through things, I need to be able to open up and vent to my wife. She is my helpmate, and I need to know that she can hold me down when I am going through.

Devotional: Men, there may be times in your marriage where you feel alone and just need that extra attention from your wife. The women in your lives will have to understand that we have a lot of different pressures on us that we face and besides GOD, they are our safe place. Most women will understand this principle and if not then pray that the woman that you are with understands this. Have those conversations about needing that safe place with her when you are going through tough times, and naturally, as a woman, she should pick those clues up and be there for you when those times arrive. If she does not have that type of discernment, pray to GOD that He reveals it to her during those times of need.

Prayer 10- (What I prayed) God, she is mad at me for asking my friend was I wrong about a situation in our marriage. She thinks I shouldn't be telling another woman our business, but I want to make sure I am not tripping in this situation. She saw the conversation, I just needed a woman's perspective, and since she doesn't want to have a conversation with me about it, I just need to make sure it is not me.

(What I should've prayed)- Father Forgive me, as the leader of this household, I should have never sought the advice from another woman in my marriage. Please forgive me because although my intentions were pure, I married my wife and not anyone else, so I need to talk about our issues with her. GOD let me understand that this destroys trust in our marriage and I have to make better decisions.

Devotional: Men, it is vital that you never bring another woman into your marriage when you are going through issues with your spouse. This is one of the quickest ways to lose the trust of your woman, and it can also be embarrassing to her when you do not know the intention of the other woman. We have to affair proof our marriages at all cost, and even if your intentions are pure, the other woman's intentions may not be. The biggest thing to understand here is that no woman should know what is going on between you and your spouse. If it gets to the point where you feel the need to involve someone else, I would defer to speak to a Pastor (if you go to church) or speak to a counselor that can help you navigate through those issues. Once you allow another woman in your marital issues, you have given the enemy something to cause division.

Prayer 11 (What I prayed) – God, she gets mad at me when I ask her to get off that damn phone.

Then, asks me what I want to talk about if she gets off the phone. She already has a negative attitude, so I don't want to speak at all. We have been sitting here all day, and all she has been doing is on that phone, I just want to throw that phone because she is always on it.

(What I should've prayed) – God, I pray that she sees that I just want to work on our communication. I feel so disconnected right now and need her to see what I feel. I pray that she understands that my love language is quality time and I just need her undivided attention. I feel lonely in this marriage, and that phone gets more attention than I do. God, help our marriage, please.

Devotional: Men, it is truly a good thing to know and understand your woman's love language. Once you can determine that along with setting boundaries and times in your marriage where you both can speak and share time with each other, the communication part will be great. Have that communication with your spouse in a positive manner if being on the phone too much becomes a problem. All parties should understand those things that cause division and ask God to direct your paths through those situations that can be resolved easily. Things like these are growing pains, and you can grow through them, but the best way to handle it is in the best positive manner as possible.

Prayer 12 (What I prayed)- God, I don't have a problem with her going out with her girlfriends, but she needed to understand that I needed her tonight. She keeps saying that her friend is "going through" and has "a lot on her plate," but does she understand that I have a lot on my plate. Hell, we have a lot on our own plates, why do I feel like I have to compete with her friends? She needs to open her eyes.

(What I should've prayed) God. Let me be a support to her as she is helping her friend that may be on the edge. Let me not be selfish with my thoughts and feelings and pray for whatever her friend is going through right now. My job as a husband is to pray for everyone who is connected to her, so let me pray for her friend as well.

Devotional: Men, I learned to ask God to reveal to her those times when our spirits should be so connected that my wife will know when I really need her. Both men and women need to understand that after God, your spouse is your first responsibility and their needs have to be met first. We wouldn't want Christ to worry about Himself and not attend to our needs when we needed Him. I would encourage both men and women to make sure that regardless who needs you, learn how to communicate and be there for each other first and everyone else falls into place. At no time should there be anyone allowed to be put over your spouse if we are going by the Bible standards. That's why the two become one flesh, being one flesh should mean that as you take care of your spouse first, you understand you are taking care of yourself.

Prayer 13 (What I prayed)- God, she is extra clingy today. She just wants me to lay in the bed with her all day, and every single time I get up, she asks me where I am going and what I am doing. As soon as I get in bed, she wants to lay on me. I don't feel like it all day, just to be laying here is not what I planned to do, maybe someone will call her and ask her to go out because I can't be in here with her all day.

(What I Should've prayed)- God, please forgive me for being selfish. Remind me that I am her covering, and I am her priest according to Your word. Today she really needs me to be around her. Let her feel my love and let me understand that she needs me despite how I feel at the moment. I prayed for us to spend quality time together and now that she needs it I am complaining. I am completely wrong God; I thank You for her.

Devotional: Men, your spouse just wants to be in your presence at times, that is something to embrace fully. This may be sporadic, or it may often be, but whenever it is, it is a reminder of how the church needs Jesus Christ. We always want Christ with us; we want him to be close to us not turning away not moving away. One of the best feelings as a husband is to have the woman you love just want to be in your presence, that is the love she has for you. We have to remember to cater and shower our wives with love still making sure we have balance and have our space, but enjoy those moments knowing that life is precious and we don't know how long we will have our spouse on this earth.

Prayer 14 (What I prayed) - God, we are sitting here having a screaming match with each other, and I am about to leave. She gets mad when I threaten to walk out that door, but I am tired of arguing with her. I don't give a damn what she has to say or what her point is right now because she isn't listening to anything that I am saying right now. If she wants to continue to scream and not respect me as the husband and talk to me, then she can go about her business, and I will go about mine.

(What I should've prayed)- God, I rebuke the enemy's attack on my marriage as the head. If we continue to yell at each other, we will not hear each other at all. I cannot lead this family if I continue to be confrontational instead of recognizing when the enemy is attacking. Let me take my wife and pray with her right now at this time so that we can destroy the satan's plan over our marriage. Satan will not destroy what God has put together.

Devotional: Men, again we have to remember to try our best to speak soft words to our wives. They are like precious flowers given to our care, and we have to care for them, so they do not wither but continue to bloom. There were times during those screaming matches where I know I could have just fell back, but it had already gotten to the point of no return. Remember to think about what is the end game in all that yelling, what purpose does it have and how will it improve your marriage? If there isn't anything positive that it will do for your marriage, then you have to find a better way of communication. Sometimes the way we communicate with our spouse is how we saw our parents handle their situations. I came from a household where yelling was a norm in the way of communication between my parents. While she came from a household where the kids never saw the parents argue in front of them. You have to manage that where it is not affecting the way you speak to your spouse and also make sure that it doesn't follow to the next generation, (your children.)

Prayer 15 (What I prayed) – God, she just found out that I was having an emotional affair with another woman. I told her time and time again that I needed to talk to her. Although she is hurt, I feel like because she was neglecting me emotionally, I had to get it from somewhere else. She doesn't understand that this other woman was there for me during a rough time in my life. She listens to me, she makes me happy every day and helps me out when I need it. She even asks me for help with some things in her life, and it feels good to be needed. My wife should have listened when I was begging her for some quality time or just to hang out with no distractions. Yes, I feel bad, but God what am I supposed to do when I told her time and time again that I needed her to LISTEN TO ME!!!!

(What I should've prayed)- God, I come to you repenting for I have sinned against You and sinned against my wife. Although there was no physical cheating, I still have done wrong, and I ask for your forgiveness. I have already asked for her forgiveness, and I did not act as a leading husband is supposed to. If I felt disconnected from her, then I should have gone to you continually in order to not to fall and please my flesh. I have no one to blame this on but myself. God, I just didn't know how to communicate to her that I really need to be able to vent to her about things, but that is still no excuse for what I did, and she has every right to be upset and hurt about it. Please soften her heart so that she knows that I feel really bad for what I did and I will do all I can to make sure that it doesn't happen again.

Devotional: Men, it is never a good idea to have a "work wife," and emotional cheating is no excuse despite what your spouse isn't doing. One thing I know is that you have to be careful on how you communicate with any female especially if they know the ends and outs of your marriage. This is another reason why you should never vent to a female about what you are going through because you can lose control. Even in my prayer, I tried to make excuses for emotional cheating, but it never has to get that far. If you feel like you are drifting so far from your spouse, have that conversation with them. Sometimes, you have to have real raw conversations about how you are feeling and pray with your spouse and GOD. The best advice I can give you is to pray with your spouse every single day, even when you are mad with them, through this prayer, it helps you remember the promise with GOD to affair proof your marriage on any level. Remember, you made vows not just to your spouse, also to GOD. So, I would encourage that if you have started any emotional cheating that you cut off all ties immediately, ask GOD for forgiveness and work your way through counseling and redemption.

Prayer 16 (What I prayed)- God, why is she sitting up here in the therapist office acting as if she hasn't done anything in this marriage to add to the strife of it. We both fell short and had to ask for forgiveness, and she came in being defensive. She needs to listen to the therapist because something has got to give. When I walk out this door, I am praying that they give her something that she can work on, on a daily basis. She needs to work on being a submissive wife and understanding what that means. Half of the battles we have are because she tries to do everything as if I am not here, doing what I have to do.

(What I should've prayed)- God, I pray that You help us both while we are getting the counseling we need to help in our marriage. I pray that I focus on those things that I need to fix for myself and that my wife gets the help she needs. Whatever her pains are God, I pray that You heal them and that You open both of our hearts so that we can get the real healing that we need.

Devotional: Men, when you are counseling remember that you are there to see how you can be a better husband. Often times, we think that the counselor is supposed to side with us and point out all the bad stuff that our spouse is doing. We want them to correct them there and now on a quick fix. If we are wise as we should be, then we should understand that our goal is to listen to the therapist, but also work on the things that we have to work on for ourselves. Couples Therapy is very vital and important and even doing a marital checkup can help you get through some underlining issues that may be present.

Prayer 17 (What I prayed) – (Late Part 1) GOD, why am I sitting here waiting for her to come pick me up? She knows damn well what time I would be here and it's cold out here. Why is it that I have to wait day after day on her picking me up as if she thinks I have time to waste? GOD, I would never have her waiting in the cold so why should I have to wait.

(What I should've prayed) God, I am frustrated, I want to stay calm and not get in the car going off, but I am mad. I pray you show my wife how important it is to be on time, how much that it shows me I am her priority.

Devotional: Men, if you are in a marriage that you only have one car for the entire family, your best bet is to do your best at working those situations out. Find out about carpooling with a male coworker (or if your wife is comfortable with a female coworker dropping you home) then that will save some issues. The both of you can actually look at carpooling options if your schedules do not permit you guys to work it out timing wise. I have seen couples with one car have difficulties as each party wanted to do their own thing at times and come and go as they please. Even in my frustration of having one car, I tried everything I could to make sure that we worked it out as a team because I did not want this to be an issue in my marriage.

Prayer 18 (What I prayed)- God, why do I feel like I am the only one saying to the kids at times when we need to be on the same page. Sometimes I feel like she just ignores what's going on because she is stuck in her world and it gets annoying. I don't want to be the parent who says no or addresses things, and she has to say something.

(What I should've prayed)- God, please let my wife understand it can be difficult being in a blended family. That my fear is that the boys won't always listen to what I am saying because I am not their biological father. They know I am only telling them stuff to teach them and protect them, but I need her to be a teammate with me on this.

Devotional: Men, blended families can be very tricky, but for the most part they can work. Even with your own kids, you and your spouse have to be on the same page as it relates to expectations from the kids, and from the other spouse on how to discipline the kids. This is one area that I would advise everyone to pray with your spouse over each one of your kids. Each of your children is different and you have to parent them different at times, something you will find out. Sometimes as men, you have an expectation of your children as it relates to household chores and how you want things done, but even in this, we have to be careful how we speak our expectations to our spouse, especially in front of the children. Do your best not to fight in front of them even in disagreement, there is always a better way.

Prayer 19 (Cell Phone Part 2) (What I prayed)- God, we are on a date, and she feel the need to pull her cell phone out every single time. Every time I say something about it again she has an issue. Why do I have to keep explaining to her that this is our time, we barely have a date night, and that is bad enough? This cell phone thing is driving me insane and I am just going to sit here nonchalant and get through this date.

(What I should've prayed)- God, what can I do? As a man, I can't take this disrespect anymore. I have done all I can to try and work this marriage out with her and I know you are big on marriage, but this is enough. How much more can I ignore the disrespect, the arguing, and everything else that comes with it? I am tired lord, but I know that through prayer we can work it out together.

Devotional: Men, one big area that we have to stay in constant prayer about is communication. There are women that are super phone users, and they do have to understand balance and marital alone time, so pray for your spouse in this area. Set the boundaries ahead of time that when you are on a date, no electronics out. Men and women, this is your time to be intimate with your spouse through conversation, and nothing should interfere with that. To those in business, you also have to set boundaries when you are spending quality time with your spouse. You can't allow money to control your marriage or allow business to get in front of your marriage. This is key in protecting your marriage as quality time is very important.

Prayer 20 (Late Part 2) (What I prayed)- God, it is now 11:30pm and I have been waiting 15 minutes at this train station in the cold. I am so angry right now, it is cold, and we have had this conversation time and time again about being on time. We live 10 minutes away from this station, why is it taking her so long to get here and leave me in this cold. When I get in this car, she better have an explanation on why I am still out here waiting.

(What I should've prayed)- God, as the man of this family I am trying to keep the peace. Even when I don't feel appreciated or respected I am trying my hardest to continue to keep the peace. Please reveal to her how I am feeling and what that does to me. Going off and yelling and arguing with her isn't going to change anything. God, this is bigger than us, and we need Your guidance on how to handle this. If not, we will not win, I will not make it through this marriage.

Devotional: Men, this can be a hard area to navigate in your marriage in a situation where your spouse may not fully grasp behaviors that maybe detrimental to the marriage. Your wife will have to understand your needs as both man and woman have to put the other needs before your own. Christ puts the needs of the church upfront as the church is His bride. As stated earlier, continue to have those tough conversations with your spouse about how to be an effective wife as while you also try to be an effective husband. No one should have to continually be put on the back burner or not considered in the manner and having one care can cause so many issues. Prayer in this area is also very vital for a successful marriage.

Prayer 21- (What I prayed) God, it's time for her guest to get the hell out of my house. I don't care how long they have been friends, but she has to go. It's like I come home and I get no love. All she does is sit down there with her friend and come up when she feels like it. I can't even get a moment with my wife and her friend has overstayed her welcome. Why am I complaining to You, God? When I just need to leave, it's issue after issue, and I am not dealing with this. I will just tell her friend she has to leave.

(What I should've prayed) God, am I wrong for feeling the way that I feel? Please let me get out of my feelings and emotions and be a better house host. We can work things out without discord, and I don't want to cause any unnecessary arguments between us.

Devotional: Men, remember that house guest should also be a topic of conversation before the marriage. In the event that you run across this issue, you always want to make sure you and your wife agree upon the person and the amount of time that they are allowed to stay in your home. As men, we try all we can to please our wife, but we have to set precedents as anyone, family included can cause division in your marriage. Your wife has to understand that you being the protector of the house want to make sure that adding an extra person can still keep the peace in your home and the minute any peace has been altered or changed that person is now a liability to the home, at that point it may be time for them to go.

Prayer 22 (What I prayed)- Dear God, I found out that she was texting someone else, but before I confront her, I need your help. I am enraged right now, and I know that I am going to react in a way that is going to be chaotic. How dare she even think about entertaining someone else after I have done all I can for this family. God she is going to feel my wrath when I see her.

(What I should've prayed) – God, if You don't intervene right now, I am not going to make it. I am ready to walk away right now, and I refuse to deal with this. I know You are telling me to stay right now, but I am not staying when she is entertaining someone else. I am ANGRY right now, but as ANGRY as I am, I have to trust You. This isn't easy, but I will do what I can.

Devotional: Men, anytime your spouse begins to emotionally cheat with someone, there has been a major disconnection and before things get out of hand in the most negative way, this is a time for talking and praying. As it says in 1 Corinthians 13: 5 love keeps no record of wrongs so this is an area where both of you can't point fingers about who did what. If you catch your wife texting or messaging another person, this is an opportunity to give her a chance to come clean. Remember that we made a vow to stick through the marriage through thickness and thin, and just like we cheat on God with other gods and things, it is our job to do everything we can to get help for the marriage. This can be a huge turning point in your marriage that needs to be addressed through communication, prayer, and definitely counseling. Once anyone allows another person in your marriage regardless whose fault it is, you can beat the enemy will do all he can to run rapid in your marriage.

Prayer 23 (What I prayed)- God, is she really mad at what I got her for Christmas when I was really giving from my heart. After all the time I spent working hard to find specific things for her, she has a whole attitude. I am never getting her anything else, and she is so ungrateful. To have a whole attitude in front of the kids, even when she gets me stuff I don't like, I act like I like it and keep it moving. She messed this whole Christmas up with her nasty attitude.

(What I should've prayed)- God, if I missed something, reveal it to me please. I am doing the best that I can as a husband and really wanted to get her something that I thought she would like. She is angry because she gave me a list, but she knows I always go above and beyond and get more. Let me not have an attitude about this situation and try to keep a positive attitude for the kids right now. Being the head of the household isn't easy at times, and it's one of those times that requires patience from me, let me show that patience.

Devotional: Men, I have learned that listening to your wife is very important as it relates to what they want at times. So often we think we got it down packed on the gift giving, but have you ever bought something, and you could tell by her response she did not like it. How do you avoid this? Sometimes, you just have to ask your wife "Baby what would you like for your birthday" It's good to be spontaneous, but sometimes just asking may help. Nothing will make her smile like you getting exactly what her heart desires.

Prayer 24 (What I prayed) God, I am not happy in this marriage at all. I come home every single day ready to get out of this thing. We just have run our course in this marriage, and she is not giving any effort to help out. This marriage is dead, there is no fire, there are no flames, it is just dead with nothing left. I can no longer give any more energy to this, I give up, God, and I just really give up.

(What I should've prayed)- God, what can I do to get rid of this feeling? I don't know where to go from here and because I am lost, how can I lead this family. We have stopped communicating and I don't know how to get back to where we should be. Teach me, Lord, how to restore this marriage, send Your Holy Spirit to guide me in this walk and help restore this marriage if it is Your will to do so.

Devotional: Men, there may be a point in your marriage when you want to throw in the towel completely. When you may have tried couples counseling, and it just did not work the way you wanted it to work. I want to encourage you to continue to seek God before throwing everything away. God's expectations are for you to work through even the hardest times in your marriage, but you don't want to just act off your emotions. Have that conversation with your spouse about how to get back to that loving place. The place you both were at the altar when you agreed to get married in the first place. Sometimes, we want to stop hurting in the marriage and it is easier to just give up but exhaust all options and make it as if divorce is not an option if you can get everything corrected.

Prayer 25- (What I prayed) GOD why is she fighting with me on moving in with my mother.

This is the time that we can be saving money for a year and get ready to buy our house, and she refuses to even budge. Right now, when we only have limited income coming in, we have to be wise GOD, and she just wants to be selfish. At this point, we have to swallow any pride we have and move in with her so that we can save money and do what we need to do.

(What I should've prayed)- God, I need Your help, financially, we are not in a place where we should be, and I need her to see that moving in with my

mom is going to help us get there. I don't want to continue to be mad at her, but God help her understand that if we are to hit our goals, this is a step in the right direction. Let her follow me as I follow You, and we trust You in this process.

Devotional: Women, this devotion goes to you because sometimes, the man sees the writing on the wall and you need to follow his lead. Men, times may get hard and money issues have been quoted as the number one cause of the divorce. If only one spouse is working or there is limited income coming in the home, have that conversation first about budgeting and cutting things financially out of your lives. If you do this and it still doesn't work then look to moving in with your parents if you have the option or a family member that it wouldn't cause tension in your marriage. Saving up for a year and working through it can help save you marriage in the long run. What you will find out is that a lot of grown adults are moving back home to save cash in a time when our country makes it hard for most families just can't afford places. Present the option to God and see if this temporary change will help your marriage, there is no shame in asking for help.

Prayer 26 (What I prayed) God, she didn't learn anything from this marriage conference that we just came from. We had such a great time and learned everything there should have been to learn about a husband and wife and still we are in the same boat. All we do is argue, fuss, yell, and I am tired of going through this same cycle with her. I know she learned some things from the wives' session and all the things that we learned together, so why is she just staying in her negative way.

(What I should've prayed) God, with the tools that we were equipped with this weekend at this marriage retreat, let us use them successfully. God, all I want to do is fix this marriage and somehow get us back on track. I feel like somewhere along the way, we lose too many battles as a married couple, and I don't know how to fix this. I figured a weekend around married couples and learning about selfless love would help fix the issues we are having in our marriage, but I was wrong. Now I need Your help and strength God, and You are the only person I can turn too.

Devotional: Men and Women, find marriage conferences you can go to that can build your marriage and give you tools to last. Once you are equipped with those tools, then you want to put them into action as they are meant to help you and build your marriage. All marriages can always be better in some area, can improve in some area as we are human and no one is perfect, there is no such thing as the perfect marriage. If you can find a good conference or retreat to go to, even if you have minimal marital problems, refreshers are always great as they can enhance your marriage on all levels. As we all know any enhancement to your marriage can make it go a long way.

Prayer 27 (What I prayed) – God, what in the world did we get baptized together as a family for if NOTHING is changing in this marriage. I thought for sure that if we got baptized with the boys and we did this as a family that things would somehow get better. I just don't understand what is going on, you gave me this family to lead, and she isn't following. How many times do we have to go over the same issues we have been having day after day, month after month, year after year. Again, I need you to fix this God because I can no longer take it.

(What I should've prayed)- God, getting baptized with the kids was a huge step for this family, and we are taking away from it. Reveal to the both of us what we are doing to contribute to what is going on with this marriage. If we have any chance to save this marriage, then lord we need Your strength to make it through. I can't do this by myself, but I will pray that You help me with the things I need to work on myself as the head of this household. In Jesus name, Amen.

Devotional: Men, as you can tell sometimes, in marriages you go through a really hard season where nothing seems to change. This is just like Christ marriage with the church in this season. Right now, no matter how consistent and patient God has been with us, we continue to stay stagnant and nongrowing in our relationship with Christ because of the many excuses that we make. What I realized is that you have to look for patterns that affect your marriage. What patterns are you displaying as the husband that are causing issues in your marriage that needs immediate addressing? Wives, what patterns are you displaying as the wife that need to be addressed? At this point in a marriage when nothing seems to be working, how often are you praying together and really trying to find those areas that need the most help from God. Sometimes if the first marriage counselor didn't work, there's nothing wrong with getting a second opinion. If your Pastor didn't work for you, ask your Pastor if he knows someone who can be neutral to you both so there is no feeling of biased in the process. You can save your marriage no matter how dark it gets; there is always light.

Prayer 28- (What I prayed) God, I decided to just sleep on the sofa for these last couple of days because I am not doing anything else until she and I can get on the same page. Why Should I be a husband to a wife who ignores everything that I try to show her and nothing works? It seems like she will call her friends and vent to them about OUR issues instead of having a husband and wife conversation with me. I know I sound like a broken record right now with my prayers, but I am tired of praying about this. If she doesn't get her act together, God, it won't be much more of a decision for me but to leave at this point.

(What I should have prayed)- God, I am hurting right now. I need to go on a fast so I can really hear from you. I want to be in line with everything that I am called to do as it relates to marriage but how can I be in the space that I am in. God, it is going to take a miracle for You to fix this marriage, but You are a miraculous God so I know if anyone can, You can.

Devotion: Men, what I learned is that it's best that you stay in the bedroom even if things are getting worse. The first thing I can tell you, sofas aren't comfortable lol, but also even if you have another bedroom in the house which you can sleep in, that is causing more division. Take over as the head and tell your wife that you guys are going to pray through this and do all you can to make it right. We get so caught in our emotions and feelings in the situation that we don't realize our disposition is huge and people on the outside can start to see it. If you have 1 or 2 couples that are near and dear to you both that can pray with you and come over as an emergency situation so that you guys can manage the situation. Going through anything by yourself is difficult but going through a rough patch as a couple by yourselves can definitely be tough.

Prayer 29 (What I prayed)- God, she and I haven't spoken to each other in a whole week. All we do is walk by each other like we don't exist. I have suggested that we go back to see a counselor, but she refuses to see one. God, why did You make me go through all of this when I am doing my part as a husband? You said if I just trusted in You and give it all to You that I would be fine. God, You said that my marriage would be fixed and fine but it isn't, and I don't feel like You are here for me. I see her laughing and smiling like life is all good, and I am here miserable trying to fix this, God I can't take this, and I don't feel like You are on my side.

(What I should've prayed)- God, I hear You telling me to completely let go and give this marriage to You. I have been fighting for so long trying to fix it myself with no luck, and in my prayer, I heard You several times say let it go and let you take control. How do I do that God, when I love her so much? I love everything about this woman, and all I want to do is make things right. We have been married going on seven years now, and I just want to continue to go on strong. We made a vow to each other to renew our vows every five years, and we didn't keep that promise. God, I trust You, and I will continue to trust You even though I don't see where this is going. I will trust in Your process and see where this goes, that's all I can do.

Devotional: Men, not speaking to your wife can be a very dangerous thing. Now I will admit, sometimes if there is a situation that requires you both to take a breather for things to calm down, then that is fine. Going more than one day of not speaking can be detrimental in restoring your marriage. If this happens, take this time to really search Christ for help. Life is too short to be mad at the person you said you wanted to spend the rest of your life with. I always wondered, how can two people who were so in love become daily enemies. Where does all the love go? Does it get buried under so much hurt that it can't be saved again or we so stuck in our ways that we aren't willing to change and forgive? What if God didn't want to forgive us for the things we did?

Prayer 30 (What I prayed) (The Final Prayer)- God, today I came home, and I saw the messages. She has been cheating on me and having an affair with her ex. I am so numb right now, I don't know what to say so tired, I'm not even angry. Nothing more to say.

(What I should've prayed) (The Final Prayer)- God, I am stepping away, in this process I need You to strengthen me, I have no strength, I have no power. I need You. I will trust whatever You tell me. In Jesus name

Devotional: Men, the only sin in the Bible that God says a man can divorce his wife for is adultery. Now physical cheating is harder to forgive than emotional cheating to some, but cheating is cheating nonetheless. When you or your spouse commits adultery, you have done the ultimate betrayal in the eyes of God. Yes, God will forgive you, but we have to be careful and not abuse His grace. How do you forgive someone that has given the best part of them, to someone else who was not you? At this point, you have the Biblical option to leave your marriage. My suggestion to you is stay only if you won't bring it up in arguments later and you can move on from it. Now that doesn't mean that it will ever go away, but it does mean you can move forward without it affecting your future dramatically. My advice also, is to seek counseling for yourself to manage through this feeling. I can tell you it becomes difficult especially if you allow it to consume your thoughts. But all in all, my encouragement is that you can get through it and allow God to help and restore your marriage.

I pray that the scriptures below will help you in your courtship and marriage journey. Please meditate on them, pray with each other, let the words of the scriptures fill your spirit.

Genesis 1:27-28, Genesis 2:24, Ephesians 4:2-3, Colossians 3:14, Ephesians 5:25-33, Mark 10:9, 1 Corinthians 13:4-8, Proverbs 3:3-4, Proverbs 31:10-12, Romans 12:10, 1 Peter 3:7, Proverbs 18:22

www.ingramcontent.com/pod-product-compliance
Lightning Source LLC
Chambersburg PA
CBHW070752050426
42449CB00010B/2437